First published 2016 by Chanelle Elana.

ISBN: 978-0-646-95061-7

Email: info@totheheartandback.com
Website: www.totheheartandback.com
Instagram: @_totheheartandback_
Facebook: www.facebook.com/totheheartandback
Publisher & Creative Director: Chanelle Elana
Illustrator: Hannah Roberts
Calligrapher: Lauren Hung
Graphic Designer: Nicol Reid
Editor: Dennis Pahos

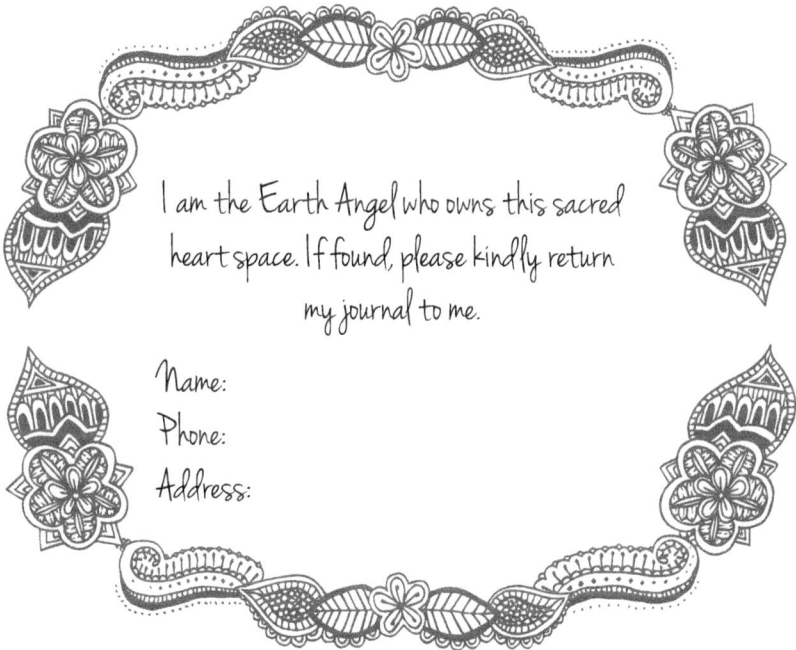

I am the Earth Angel who owns this sacred heart space. If found, please kindly return my journal to me.

Name:

Phone:

Address:

Dear Earth Angel

Thank You for purchasing 'To the Heart and Back', your guide to awakening, expressing and defining your purpose in life. To the Heart and Back will empower and inspire you to choose Love over fear and honour your true Self. It will develop your ability to harness your inner strength so that you begin to lead a vibrant and spirited life filled with Love, creativity, expression, clarity and colour.

To the Heart and Back is an idea, a concept, story, movement, an adventure, come from the ether - From my Heart to Yours.

I always had an urge for more. I knew I had more to give and a message to spread far and wide. I discarded routine in favour of risk and courage. I searched within and found a part of me that felt protected, safe and excited for the next chapter of my life and what lay ahead.

I always felt an inner calling to influence, motivate, move and inspire. Then one day after meditating, the idea came to me - I want to create a journal of my own. A journal designed to awaken the free spirit within, to ignite creativity, to cleanse and transform Hearts.

Since the age of twelve, I've been recording my thoughts and feelings in an attempt to make sense of my life. I still have boxes of journals that I treasure - I've kept them all these years. I Love anything handwritten, indeed anything handmade. Lovingly crafted, this is a journal you can hold, touch, feel and cherish. With a nostalgic return to the handwritten, it is a space for you to write down, capture and reflect upon your innermost thoughts for years to come.

I fall in love with words, especially when they speak to my Heart. Through my words, I intend to share my Heart and Soul so that I may open yours.

Writing has always taken me to another world, another dimension, a place where creatives, dreamers and free-spirits all meet and conspire to elevate you.

Open your Heart to write and express your most sacred thoughts and ideas, giving them your energy and real potential. Let your thoughts unfold with no judgement on what is right or wrong.

To the creative Souls who write, draw or create - I am with you. To the sensitive Souls who feel everything deeply - I am with you. To those who do not recognise their creative potential, allow To the Heart and Back to awaken your unique gift, we all have one.

Realise your passion and dream. Believe in yourself. Dream it, believe it, follow it and then run with it. We all have a place, a story, a dream and a destiny if we allow it to unfold. Believe, let go, and trust.

To the Heart and Back will inscribe a message to keep Love in its purest form in your Heart Always. It will bring you closer to your true Self. Love is all there is within and all around you.

I ask the Universe to be your guide, your teacher and your companion. May it lead you to new adventures, new beginnings and bless everything you do.

Love,

Chanelle Elana

Xx

Dedicated to Maree Matic

"My wish for you is that you come to see yourself the way I and others see you, that you recognise how much you offer and have to offer, that you begin to have an even deeper love affair with yourself and all of life."

– Maree Matic

Born unto Gaia – 6th September 1971
Returned to the Light – 20th August 2014

I honour who you were when you walked the Earth and the incredible Energy you've become.

I'll see you on the other side, my beautiful butterfly.

Xx

I am all for Love that is content, creative and aligned to grace - Love that is a pure and guiding force in life, facilitating healing when bruised and shattered, when fragile and broken.

When I opened up and wrote about my hurt, I began a journey towards finding my true Self and inner-strength. It is how I was able to re-shape my life. Perhaps writing regularly in a journal is the beginning of transforming and renewing your life.

Over the years I have met people who have loved and challenged me and others who rejected who I was. All of those who were destined to cross my path taught me more about myself. I have found a lesson in all the times that I have been let down. Despite this, I open my arms to Love and the world.

Be comfortable with who you are and know that you are enough. We are free to let go of anything that doesn't serve us. Trust in the power of attraction, emit positive energy into the Universe and anything that you have ever wanted may be yours.

About Chanelle Elana

A Gypsy Goddess with feathers in her hair and an open, loving Heart

A Creative with a passion for writing, art, music and dance.

A Bohemian wanderer with a yearning for adventure and freedom.

A Free Spirit with a thirst for knowledge, spiritual growth and self-development

A lover of nature and naturopathy, astrology and anything organic or handmade.

A true Libra who believes in love, harmony and balance.

She rises with the morning sun and is drawn to its horizon, with her day filled with meditation, yoga, reading and writing.

By night she yearns for the moonlight, casting its shadow over the city sprawl as an urban adventure awaits her.

All My Love and Gratitude

It all began as a solitary journey, just the Universe and I. Then, slowly but surely, my tribe began to extend itself to encompass all of those who contributed to the creation of 'To the Heart and Back'.

To my beautiful family and friends - I love you dearly and grateful for your love, support and guidance. You helped me believe in myself to achieve my dream.

To all my collaborators - I thank the Universe for bringing you all, just at the right times. I am incredibly thankful for your contribution.

With each new dawn, a new idea arises.

I open my Heart
I love
I trust
I let go
I forgive
I forget
I am happy
I am grateful

To do this,
I surrender

I let go of fear
I let go of judgement
I let go of anger
I let go of envy
I let go of jealousy
I let go of frustration

I am love
I am free
I am content
I am well
I am healthy
I am vibrant
I am joy

I am responsible for my actions
I am free to live and to Love
I am wealthy and abundant on every level
I am the Creator of my life

I am open
I am compassionate
I am forgiving

Take this new day, seize the opportunities,
see the light and be open to all the possibilities.

−Chanelle Elana

Xx

Ignite
my
Gypsy Heart

— Chanelle Elana

We come to Gaia to love, share and grow on every conceivable level.
We come to feed our souls, reflect, and learn from our experiences.
- Chanelle Elana

The Universe has a plan for you. If you trust and allow it to unfold,
you will achieve more than you ever thought was possible.
- Chanelle Elana

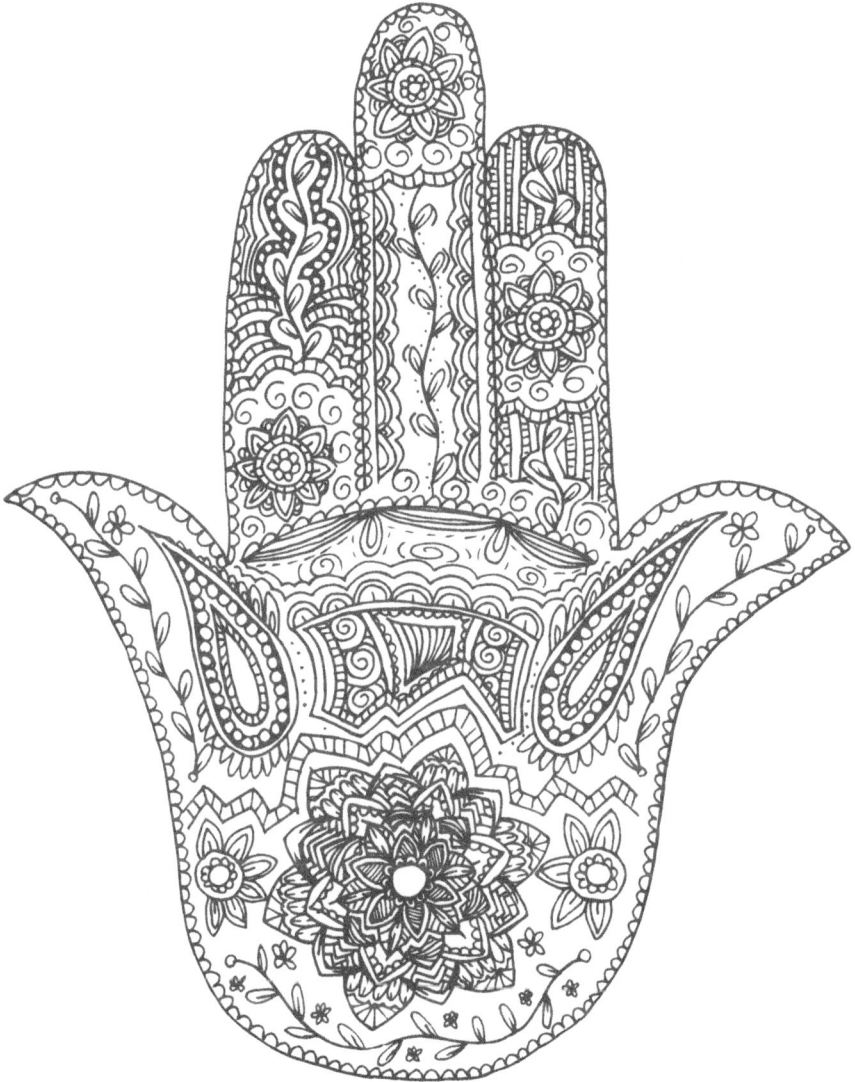

I believe in a higher power, energy, spirit, an intelligence
- one that is supportive and loving.
- Chanelle Elana

to the ♡ and back

to the ♡ and back

Dear Universe, you are my friend and guide.
I trust and know you have my best interest at Heart.
I believe wholeheartedly I am loved and supported.
- Chanelle Elana

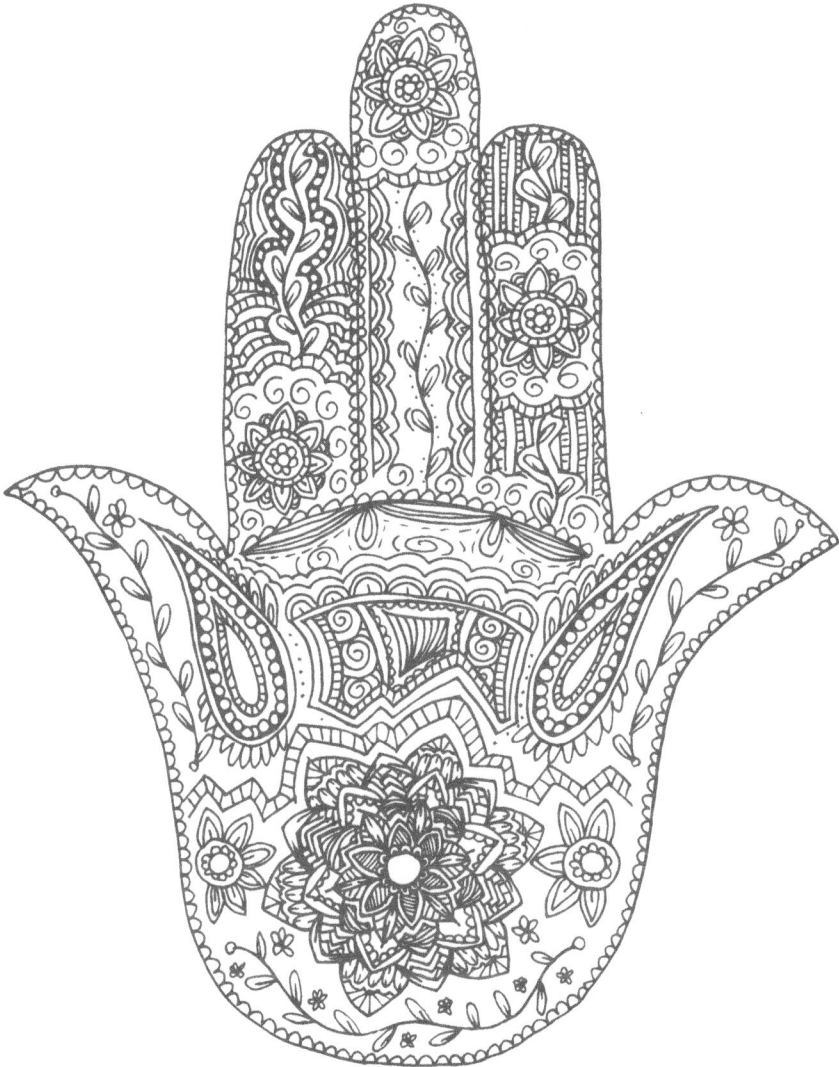

The Hamsa Hand is a universal sign of protection that represents blessings, power and strength.

to the ♡ and back

to the ♡ and back

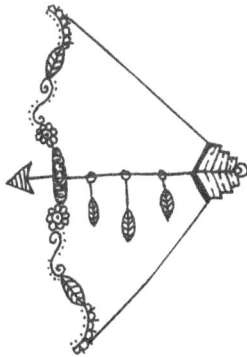

Sometimes the things we want most are not conducive to our growth. By bringing ourselves to the present moment, we become less dependent on the result and let the Universe show us a different, often better way.

— Chanelle Elana

to the ♡ and back

to the ♡ and back

I am open to new experiences, possibilities and adventures.
All the Universe has to offer!
- Chanelle Elana

I thank the Universe for today.
My Heart is open and forgiving.
- Chanelle Elana

to the ♡ and back

to the ♡ and back

We are responsible for how we feel, the quality of our energy
and how we project it. It shapes every experience
and filters our perception of reality.
- Chanelle Elana

I'm a
dreamer
and
believer
in
love and magic

— Chanelle Elana

Dreamcatchers filter out bad dreams and only allow for good thoughts to enter our minds. They symbolise strength and unity.

Learn to listen and trust your intuition - your Higher Self
speaking to you with messages of truth, guidance and wisdom.
- Chanelle Elana

to the ♡ and back

to the ♥ and back

Jar of dreams

Jar of dreams

Ultimately, we all need to live our truth, pursue what we love
and fulfil our deep-seated passion. So, go ahead, do it
- Chanelle Elana

Dark days
don't
Linger for
long

— Chanelle Elana

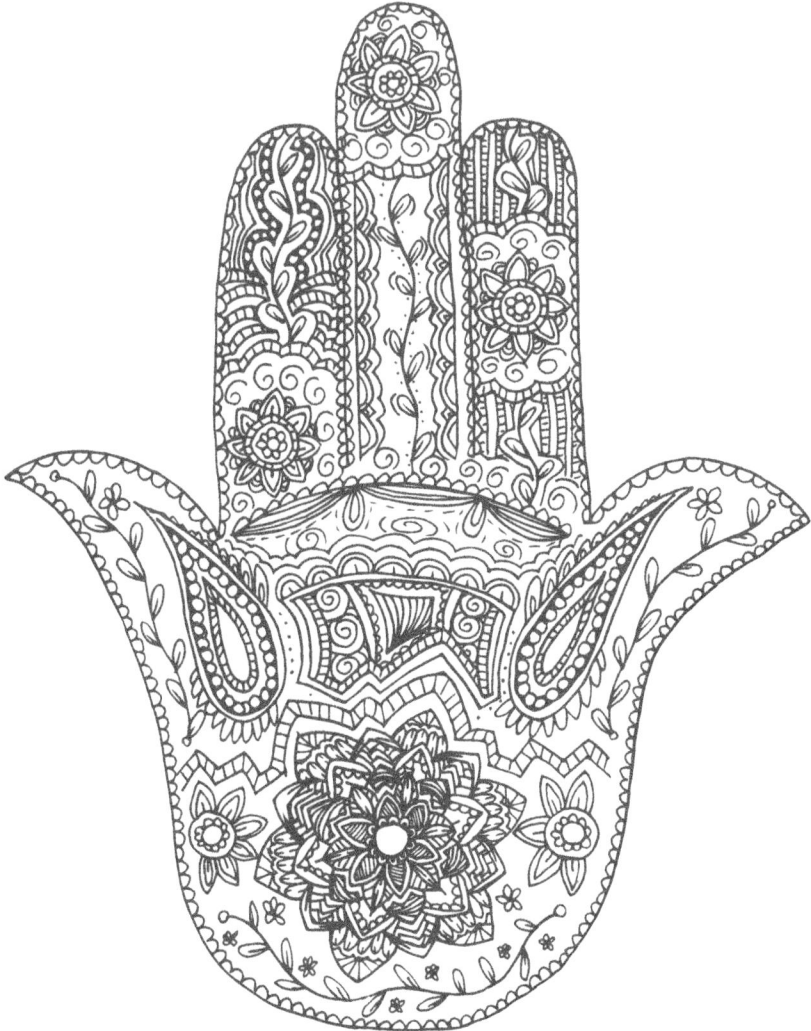

Everyone is entitled to their opinion but don't give up your dignity and surrender to other people's judgement.
Do what you love.
Write, draw, sing, paint, whatever you feel your calling is.
Believe, let go and trust. Most of all, live your life the way you want, not in the shadow of other people's opinions or expectations.
- Chanelle Elana

We are more than what we think we are.
Self-belief is the essence of success.
- Chanelle Elana

to the ♡ and back

to the ♥ and back

At times, we may not be the best version of ourselves but the more we learn, the more refined we become. When we are open to change, we evolve and unlock our potential.
- Chanelle Elana

Allow yourself to address your fears - write them down
and let them go. Free your mind and be open to change.
We then find our strength, wisdom and authentic 'Self'.
- Chanelle Elana

At times, we may not be the best version of ourselves but the more we learn, the more refined we become. When we are open to change, we evolve and unlock our potential.
- Chanelle Elana

Allow yourself to address your fears - write them down
and let them go. Free your mind and be open to change.
We then find our strength, wisdom and authentic 'Self'.
- Chanelle Elana

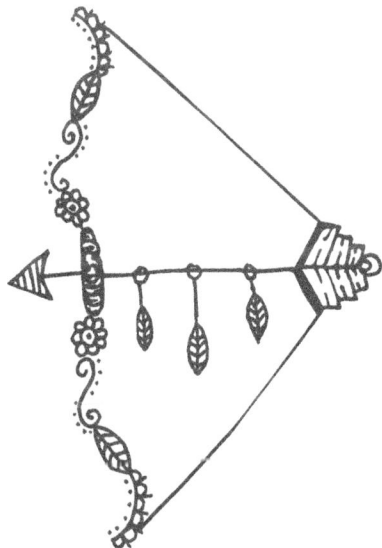

to the ♡ and back

to the ♡ and back

☮ » ♡ « ☮

Our internal dialogue and the negative emotions that we hold onto
can be a contributing factor to any ailment of the mind and body.
It is why it is crucial to let go of any negative attachments
to the past or present.
People who are not able to forgive are hard on themselves and others
- they close their minds to opportunities and growth.
Energetically, this creates a low vibration (frequency)
with a real denseness to one's energy.
We only hurt ourselves if we choose not to let go and it stops us
from moving on with our lives.
- Chanelle Elana

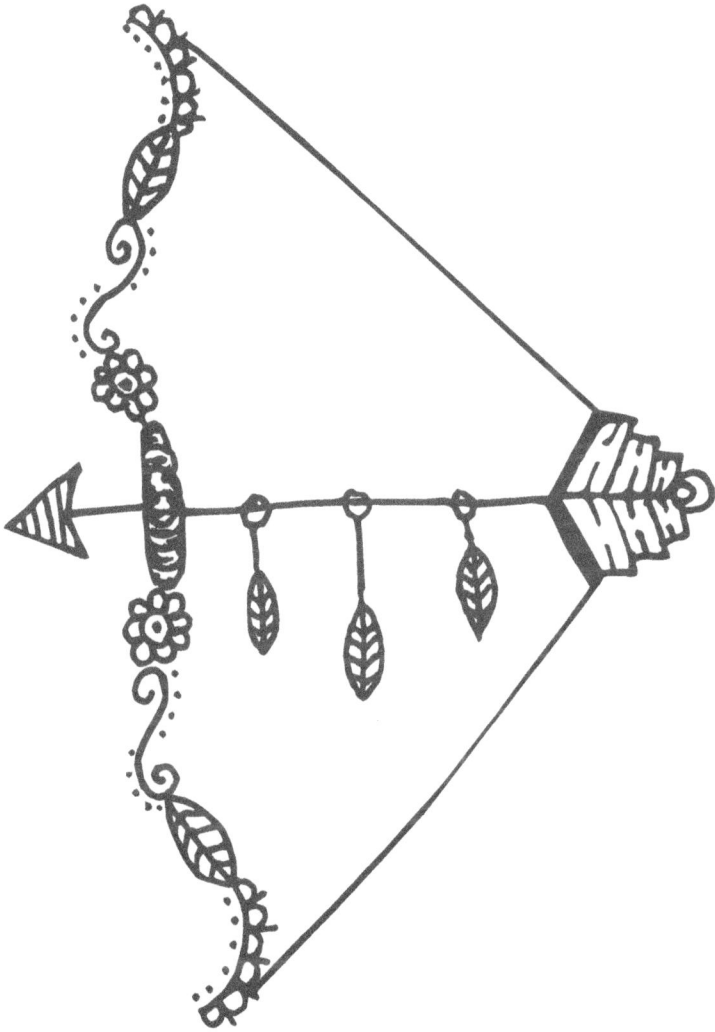

Rejection hurts but it can make you stronger.
Life is a series of lessons.
- Chanelle Elana

to the ♡ and back

to the ♥ and back

Our thoughts are energy - they can be positive or negative, nurturing or damaging. We have a choice to engage or detach.
- Chanelle Elana

Take time out to reflect why you may not be living life to the fullest. Be open to new experiences, possibilities and adventures. We don't know what life has installed for us and we can never be fully prepared.

See every day as a new beginning and an opportunity to make positive changes.

Let go of yesterday's failures and to-do lists. The time is now. The present moment is all we have.

As hard as change can be, when we confront it with courage,
we unlock our potential for growth.
We have the power to overcome life's challenges - and when we do
- we find a new sense of determination and capacity for change.

− Chanelle Elana

What does it mean to be authentic?
To be authentic is brave, attractive and heals the Soul.
When we are our true selves, we expand and grow.
It is empowering to conquer our fears and acknowledge our strengths.

Honesty is the way forward - it provides a potential for growth.
We all have fears- some greater than others - but on the flip side
of fear is Love. We are a work in progress.
Love encompasses compassion and understanding that is
the essence of our Being.

– Chanelle Elana

to the ♡ and back

to the ♡ and back

☮ ≫ ♡ ≪ ☮

I am love, I am grateful.

Make it a priority to find inner peace and self-acceptance.
- Chanelle Elana

I accept myself for all that I am and all that I have to offer. All the experiences I've had up until this point in my life have shaped the person I am. Today, I choose acceptance of my past, present and who I am becoming.

- Chanelle Elana

to the ♡ and back

to the ♡ and back

☮ ≫ ♡ ≪ ☮

☮ ≫ ♡ ≪ ☮

When we find ourselves alone on our journey, we reflect and learn
to love ourselves. We learn to appreciate who we are and understand
that we are enough, just as we are.
- Chanelle Elana

Ask yourself, how you can achieve balance in your life?
There is no right or wrong answer. We are in a time of information
overload so achieving and maintaining balance can be challenging.
We forget to disconnect from the 'external' and take time out
to self-care. It is crucial to make this a priority.
- Chanelle Elana

to the ♡ and back

to the ♡ and back

☮ » ♡ « ☮

Yin and Yang represent duality.
It signifies the unity between masculine and feminine energies.
It is a spiritual reminder that balance between light and darkness
provides a holistic approach to living a meaningful life.

Don't feel the need to live up to others' standards and expectations. Harness your inner strength and leave behind what no longer serves you. The choice is yours.
- Chanelle Elana

What is important to you? Who do you want to be?
Someone who lives a limited life because they're too afraid to take
a risk - or someone who is brave and lives their truth?
- Chanelle Elana

to the ♡ and back

to the ♥ and back

☮ » ♡ « ☮

Happiness and inner peace come from within by having an appreciation of Self. We often blame others for how we feel, when they do not act the way we expect or want them to. True love is to share your doubts, fears and insecurities with your significant other.
- Chanelle Elana

Do you feel worthy of love?
Has anything happened to you that has made you feel undeserving?
Make peace with your past so it will no longer have a hold over you.
- Chanelle Elana

to the ♡ and back

to the ♥ and back

Believe
Let Go
and
Trust

— Chanelle Elana

There is a spark in all of us that ignites our burning ambitions.

Keep your Heart kind, your mind present, and spirit thirsty.
- Chanelle Elana

to the ♡ and back

to the ♡ and back

The lotus flower is a symbol of enlightenment and detachment.
It represents our journey out of the darkness and into the light.

We are responsible for everything we feel.
In understanding what makes us tick, it can help our relationships,
including the one with ourselves.
We resist opening up to others because of our fear of judgement.
We worry about being perceived as weak.
We wear a mask and become who others want us to be.
What if they don't love me for who I am?
In doing this, we hide our authentic Self.
There is beauty in our imperfections.

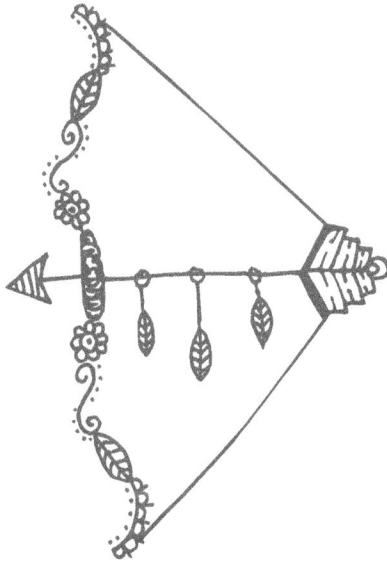

We find inner peace by acknowledging and sharing our scars
and wounds. In sharing, we immediately diffuse the power
they have over us.
There is always a different way to see things.
By being open and honest, relationships can grow
and become more meaningful.

– Chanelle Elana

to the ♡ and back

to the ♡ and back

☮ ≫ ♡ ≪ ☮

What is it that you seek? What is it you desire?
I'm craving for more than what meets the eye.
What is beyond the physical?
It goes beyond the shell, the exterior.
It's a feeling, energy, light - rejecting material,
wealth and pieces of gold and silver.
It's my Soul recognising your Soul. It goes beyond the senses.
An unspoken connection and we're speaking the same language.
I seek this not just in you but beyond the realm of
the physical world.
A moment of clarity and a sense of inner peace.
The intricate and delicate beauty of our surroundings, of what we
call Earth. At one with the universe and love that is present.
- Chanelle Elana

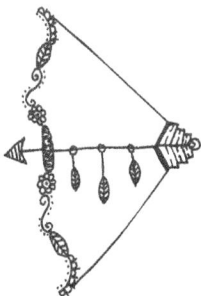

Gravitate to people who inspire, motivate, encourage and love you for who you are and all that you stand for.
Life is better when surrounded by people who understand you.
Everything happens for a reason. You attract people on the same wavelength when you allow them to come into your life.
People who are meant to be in your life will always find a way back, no matter how far they wander.
- Chanelle Elana

to the ♡ and back

to the ♡ and back

Treasure the people you have in your life.
Love them and don't hold back.
Those who come and go are meant to,
when they leave, send them love.
- Chanelle Elana

Be open to seeing the good in others and resist making judgements.
Let go of finding faults, or the need to have opinions.
- Chanelle Elana

to the ♡ and back

to the ♡ and back

Keep the power of Love in your Heart.
Love is all that matters - we cannot deny this truth.
· Chanelle Elana

to the ♡ and back

to the ♡ and back

Mandala in Sanskrit means 'circle' or 'centre', representing both the visible world around us and the invisible one inside ourselves. It conveys wholeness and a model for life itself. It is a cosmic diagram and force, connecting us to the infinite.

Mandalas engage the mind to cease chattering thoughts and enable the observer to access higher consciousness. They disengage our analytical mind and allow our creative selves to run free.

A mandala is an energetic tool that can serve us on our spiritual journey. It symbolises order, unity, and harmony.

Learn something new every day.
Play. Dance. Sing. Love. Cry. Scream. Do it all.
Laugh. Meditate. Forgive. Be considerate.
Cultivate gratitude. Love unconditionally.
Travel. Explore. Say yes. Face your fears.
Appreciate life. Appreciate each other.
Speak your truth. Be kind. Stay humble.
Take a chance. Take risks.
Open your mind. Open your heart.
Own your story. Don't wait.
Change the world. Chase the sun. Watch a sunset.
Run on the beach. Turn your phone off.
Write someone a love letter.
Send flowers to someone special unexpectedly. Be gentle.
Learn an instrument. Write. Draw.
Go to a park and play on the swings. Hug a tree.
Hug someone every day. Write a love letter to yourself.
Let go of the past. Take action.

— Chanelle Elana